W9-CBH-557

UNDERSEA SCHOOL

Disney · PIXAR

FINDING NEMO

Go Fish!
All About Fins, Gills, Scales, and More!

by Adrienne Mason

Scholastic Inc.

New York · Toronto · London · Auckland · Sydney
Mexico City · New Delhi · Hong Kong · Buenos Aires

Cover Designer: Aruna Goldstein
Interior Designer: Julia Sarno
Interior illustrations by Yancey Labat

Photo Credits:
Page 11: (ocean sunfish) © Stephen Frink/Corbis; (pygmy goby) © David B. Fleetham/SeaPics.com; (tarpon) © Masa Ushioda/SeaPics.com.
Page 14: (background yellow back fusilier & anchovies) © Rene Frederick/Photodisc Red (RF)/Getty Images; (catfish) John G. Shedd/Visuals Unlimited.
Page 15: (background yellow back fusilier & anchovies) © Rene Frederick/Photodisc Red (RF)/Getty Images.
Page 16: (background-mahognay snapper) © Rene Frederick/Photodisc Red (RF)/Getty Images.
Page 17: (background-mahognay snapper) © Rene Frederick/Photodisc Red (RF)/Getty Images; (flying fish) © Doug Perrine/SeaPics.com; (mudskipper) Brian Rogers/Visuals Unlimited.
Page 19: (background) © Michael Aw/Photodisc Green (RF)/Getty Images; (yellowfin tuna) © Bill Curtsinger/National Geographic/Getty Images; (starry flounder) Daniel Gotshall/Visuals Unlimited; (pipefish) © Mark Conlin/SeaPics.com.
Page 20: (background) © Michael Aw/Photodisc Green (RF)/Getty Images; (collared butterfly fish) © Louise Murray/Taxi/Getty Images: (garibaldi) © James Gritz/Photodisc Blue (RF)/Getty Images.
Page 21: (background-tropical fish over reef) © Digital Vision (RF)/Getty Images; (shark denticles) © Will Schubert/SeaPics.com.
Page 22: (background-tropical fish over reef) © Digital Vision (RF)/Getty Images; (stingray) © Phillip Colla/SeaPics.com; (sawfish) © Doug Perrine/SeaPics.com.
Page 23: (background-tropical fish over reef) © Digital Vision (RF)/Getty Images; (whale shark) © James D. Watt/SeaPics.com; (lamprey) © Jonathan Bird/SeaPics.com; (hagfish) Christine Ortlepp/Visuals Unlimited.
Page 24: (clown triggerfish) © Gregory Ochocki/SeaPics.com; (pygmy sea horse) © Franco Banfi/SeaPics.com; (scorpion fish) © Mark Conlin/SeaPics.com; (peacock flounder) © DR & TL Schrichte/SeaPics.com.
Page 25: (spotfin butterfly fish) © Mike Kelly/Image Bank/Getty Images; (damselfish) © Doug Perrine/SeaPics.com; (cleaner wrasse) © James D. Watt/SeaPics.com.
Page 26: (clown fish) © Frank & Joyce Burek/Photodisc Green (RF)/Getty Images; (parrot fish) © Marc Chamberlain/SeaPics.com.
Page 27: (porcupine fish) © Digital Vision (RF)/Getty Images ; (surgeonfish) Robert Myers/Visuals Unlimited; (lionfish) © Georgette Douwma/Digital Vision (RF)/Getty Images; (boxfish)© Doug Perrine/SeaPics.com; (school of salmon) © Bill Curtsinger/National Geographic/Getty Images.
Page 28: (frogfish) Steven Norvich/Visuals Unlimited; (parrot fish) © Jeff Rotman/Image Bank/Getty Images; (triggerfish) © Ian Cartwright/Photodisc Green (RF)/Getty Images.
Page 29: (trumpetfish) © DR & TL Schrichte/SeaPics.com; (torpedo ray) © Phillip Colla/SeaPics.com; (archerfish) Steven Dalton/Photo Researchers.
Page 30: (jawfish) © A & A Ferrari/SeaPics.com; (damselfish) © Gary Bell/SeaPics.com.
Page 31: (rockfish) © Masa Ushioda/SeaPics.com; (egg case) © Doug Perrine/SeaPics.com; (salmon eggs) © Jeff Mondragon/SeaPics.com; (Siamese fighting fish) © DK Limited/Corbis.
Page 32: (background-scuba diver along ocean floor) © Royalty-Free/Corbis; (viperfish) © Gregory Ochocki/SeaPics.com; (anglerfish) © Gregory Ochocki/SeaPics.com; (gulper eel) © Doc White/SeaPics.com.
Page 33: (background-scuba diver along ocean floor) © Royalty-Free/Corbis; (black sea dragon) © Doc White/SeaPics.com; (hatchetfish)© Doc White/SeaPics.com.
Page 34: (background-fishes in coral cave) © Stephen Frink/Corbis; (ratfish) © Brandon Cole/Corbis; (rat) © Royalty-Free/Corbis; (frogfish) © Robert Yin/Corbis; (frog) © Digital Vision (RF); (cowfish) © James Martin/Image Bank/Getty Images; (cows) © Dinodia Photo Library/Brand X Pictures (RF)/Getty Images; (elephant fish) © Rudie Kuiter/SeaPics.com; (elephant) © Royalty-Free/Corbis.
Page 35: (sea dragon) © Darryl Torckler/Stone/Getty Images; (angelfish) © Lawson Woods/Corbis; (shrimpfish) © Yoshi Hirata/SeaPics.com; (moray eel) © Masa Ushioda/SeaPics.com; (yellowtail kingfish) © Richard Herrmann/SeaPics.com; (sea urchin) © Darryl Torckler/Taxi/Getty Images; (rock crevices) © Don Klumpp/Image Bank/Getty Images; (open ocean) © Ihoko Saito/Toshiyuki Tajima/Dex Image (RF)/Getty Images; (seaweed) © Andre Seale/SeaPics.com; (coral reef) © Joshua Singer/Image Bank/Getty Images.
Page 36: (catfish) © James D. Watt/SeaPics.com.
Page 37: (background-golden damselfish) © Georgette Douwma/Digital Vision (RF)/Getty Images.
Page 38: (sea dragon) © Darryl Torckler/Stone/Getty Images; (angelfish) © Lawson Woods/Corbis; (shrimpfish) © Yoshi Hirata/SeaPics.com; (moray eel) © Masa Ushioda/SeaPics.com; (yellowtail kingfish) © Richard Herrmann/SeaPics.com; (sea urchin) © Darryl Torckler/Taxi/Getty Images; (rock crevices) © Don Klumpp/Image Bank/Getty Images; (open ocean) © Ihoko Saito/Toshiyuki Tajima/Dex Image (RF)/Getty Images; (seaweed) © Andre Seale/SeaPics.com; (coral reef) © Joshua Singer/Image Bank/Getty Images.

No part of this publication may be reproduced or stored in a retrieval system, or transmitted in any form or by any means, electronic, mechanical, photocopying, recording, or otherwise, without written permission of the publisher. For information regarding permission, write to Disney Licensed Publishing, 500 S. Buena Vista St., Burbank, CA 91521.

Copyright © 2005 by Disney Enterprises, Inc./Pixar Animation Studios

Published by Scholastic Inc., 557 Broadway, New York, NY 10012, by arrangement with Disney Licensed Publishing. SCHOLASTIC, UNDERSEA SCHOOL, and associated logos are trademarks and/or registered trademarks of Scholastic Inc.

ISBN 0-439-79883-3

12 11 10 9 8 7 6 5 4 3 2 1   5 6 7 8 9 10/0

Printed in the U.S.A.
First Scholastic printing, June 2005

Table of Contents

Get ready for a Fin-tastic Adventure!

Nemo
clown fish

HI, I'm Nemo! Welcome back to Undersea School! Are you ready to learn more about my friends with fins? We're going to explore the world of fish, which includes Dory, Tad, Bruce, me, my dad, and lots of my other friends!

> Don't forget about me! I'm a fish, too.

Did you know that there are more than 30,000 different kinds of fish? You'll meet all kinds of fish in this book, including:

- fish that walk.

- fish that puff up like a balloon.

- fish that light up like flashlights.

- and fish with swords on their snouts!

Sheldon
sea horse

> Hey, I can count to 30,000! One, two…where was I? One, two…

Dory
blue tang

8

You can hold onto my lucky fin, but I'm sure you'll be able to swim along just fine during our ocean adventure. After all, you have some of the same things that most fish have: a backbone, two eyes, a mouth....

Marlin
clown fish

...and a great sense of humor!

How would you describe a fish? Even though there are lots of different fish in the sea, they all share some characteristics. Almost all fish:

- live in water (freshwater or salt water).

- breathe using organs called gills.

- have scales.

- swim using fins.

- have a backbone.

Let's take a closer look at what it takes to be a fish. Flap your flippers and swim along with me!

Chapter 1: The Fishy Files

Bones and Fins and Gills...Oh, My!

Let's take a peek inside to see what makes a fish a fish.

Fish are cold-blooded. This means that their body temperature is the same as the water they swim in. (You are warm-blooded. Your body stays warm even when you're swimming in cool water.)

Most fish have backbones and hard bony skeletons, just like you do. That's why we call them "bony fish." Almost all of the fish in the ocean are bony fish. (You'll meet some fish that don't have bony skeletons on pages 21 to 23.)

Fish use gills to breathe. A flap of skin covers the gills to protect them from being damaged. We'll learn all about how gills work on page 13.

salmon

Scales cover a fish's body and protect it like a coat of armor. Scales overlap just like shingles on the roof of a house.

Most fish have pairs of fins that they use to swim and keep their balance. You'll learn more about fins on page 16.

Most fish have a swim bladder. Air is pumped into the bladder when the fish wants to go up. Air goes out of the bladder when the fish wants to go down.

Now that you know some fish fundamentals, let's take an up-close look at a few of my big and small fishy friends!

The ocean sunfish is the largest **bony fish** in the world. It can be as long as a van. And it gets that big just by eating jellyfish!

pygmy goby

The goby is one of the smallest fish in the world. It's about the size of the word *goby*!

ocean sunfish

tarpon

The tarpon has very large **scales** that cover its body. One scale can be larger than a U.S. quarter.

CLOWNING AROUND!

Q: Why is it so easy to weigh fish?

A: Because they have their own scales!

Something's Fishy

Did you ever wonder why fish are slimy when you touch them? Yup, we're all slippery characters. This slime acts like a protective blanket that keeps our skin clean and healthy. It also makes it easy for us to slip through the water.

Gill
moorish idol

stories in the scales

Fish scales have tales to tell! You can tell how old a fish is by counting the rings on its scales. One set of far-apart rings combined with one set of close-together rings equals one year. Scientists can also tell whether a fish was affected by disease, starvation, or pollution by studying the rings.

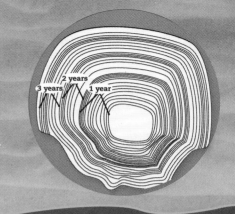

3 years 2 years 1 year

Sandy Plankton says that people who study fish are called *icky-ologists.*

That's a Mouthful, Mate!

Sandy Plankton is almost right. People who study fish are called *ichthyologists* (ICK-thee-all-oh-jists).

gulping with gills

When you take a big gulp of air, you're breathing in the oxygen that your body needs to survive. All animals, on land and in water, need oxygen. But fish, like me, can't breathe air. Instead, we use organs called *gills* to get oxygen out of the water. Want to know how this works? Let's take a look at a fish's gills.

BRUCE
great white shark

12

1. To breathe, a fish opens its mouth to let water in.

2. The water flows past its gills. Stiff spines or hooks, called gill rakers, catch big food or other things in the water that might damage its delicate gills. A fish's gills are filled with blood. When water flows over the gills, the blood absorbs the oxygen. Then the gills are filled with oxygen-rich blood. The fish's heart pumps that oxygen-rich blood around its body, keeping it alive.

gill rakers

3. Finally, the gill cover opens to let the water back out.

Cool! Fish use hooks to catch food, just like fishermen do! But fish catch food they *don't* want to eat.

Tad
butterfly fish

CLOWNING AROUND!

Q: What did the fish say to his girlfriend?

A: You're the *gill* of my dreams.

13

Chapter 2: Smells Fishy to Me!

Did you ever wonder if fish *see, smell, taste, hear,* or *feel* just like people do? Let's take a closer look at how fish sense their watery world.

Eye See You

Many fish have excellent vision. A fish's eyes work something like yours, but most fish are better able to see underwater and in the dark. You'll never see a fish blink, wink, or close its eyes. Unlike you, a fish doesn't have eyelids. (You blink to keep your eyes moist. Since fish live in water, they don't have to!)

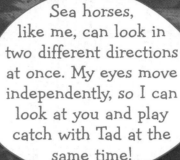

Sea horses, like me, can look in two different directions at once. My eyes move independently, so I can look at you and play catch with Tad at the same time!

Super Sniffers

Fish use their good sense of smell to find food, as well as other fish. Like you, fish have two nostrils. Water flows through the nostrils. This is how fish smell things in the sea.

catfish

Tastes Kind of Fishy

You use taste buds on your tongue to taste food. Fish have taste buds, too, but they're not just in their mouths. Taste buds can be on a fish's head, fins, tail, or even whiskers! Catfish "taste" with the whisker-like growths on their chin.

Fishy, Can You "Ear" Me?

You won't see big, fleshy earlobes, like yours, on fish, but they do have ears. Like you, fish use their ears for hearing and balance. Ears pick up sound vibrations, or sound waves, that travel through the water.

Touchy, Feely Fishy

On each side of its body, a fish has a special tube called a lateral line. A lateral line is filled with fluid and tiny cells that allow fish to feel movement, or vibrations, in the water. So, if a predator is approaching, the fish will be able to see and *feel* it coming. Fish can also use their lateral lines to detect prey. You can see the lateral line in the fish below.

lateral line

rockfish

Now you know a little bit about how we survive in our watery world. Are you ready to learn how floppy (and frustrating!) life would be without fins? Grab onto my lucky fin and let's find out!

Chapter 3: Swimming Like a Fish

Fish don't have arms or legs, but they do have *fins* that help them move through the water. Without fins, it would be impossible to swim. Fins also keep fish from rolling over. Let's take a closer look at a fish's fins.

These fins keep a fish balanced and straight so it doesn't roll over.

These fins are found on each side of a fish's body and are used for turning, backing up, and stopping.

rockfish

The tail fin is a fish's power fin. A fish swishes this fin from side to side to push forward through the water.

S...S...S...Swimming

Did you know that fish make an S-shape when they swim? Fish use their muscles to move their heads from side to side. This "wave" of movement continues down their bodies to their tails, which make large swings. This powerful back-and-forth motion moves fish forward.

CLOWNING AROUND!

Q: Why did the fish keep rolling over in bed?

A: Its fins fell asleep!

Fish that Fly and Fish that Walk

Almost all fish can swim, but there are also fish that can fly or even walk!

flying fish

Flying fish can move their tails up and down about 50 times a second! This gives them the speed they need to leap out of the water. Then, they spread their fins out like wings, and glide through the air. Flying fish can glide farther than the length of a football field!

mudskipper

The mudskipper lives in shallow swamps. It can come right out of the water and scurry on land, using the fins on its chest like crutches!

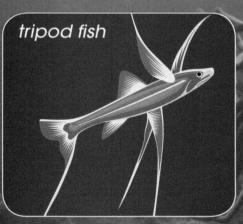
tripod fish

The tripod fish can prop itself up using long stilt-like growths on its fins.

Are you ready to take a break? Let's swim on over to the next page for some Fishy Fun!

BIRD'S-EYE VIEW

Nigel
pelican

When I see a flying fish gliding, I often see another fish swimming in the ocean right under it. Flying fish leap out of the water to get away from other fish that want to eat them.

FISHY FUN: Fishy Look-alikes

Hey...something here looks really fishy! The fish in each of the three groups below may look alike. But there are really only two fish in each group that are exactly the same. With your super-sharp undersea vision, search for the twin triggerfish, sea horses, and manta rays. Can you find them? *(When you think you've found them, turn to page 38!)*

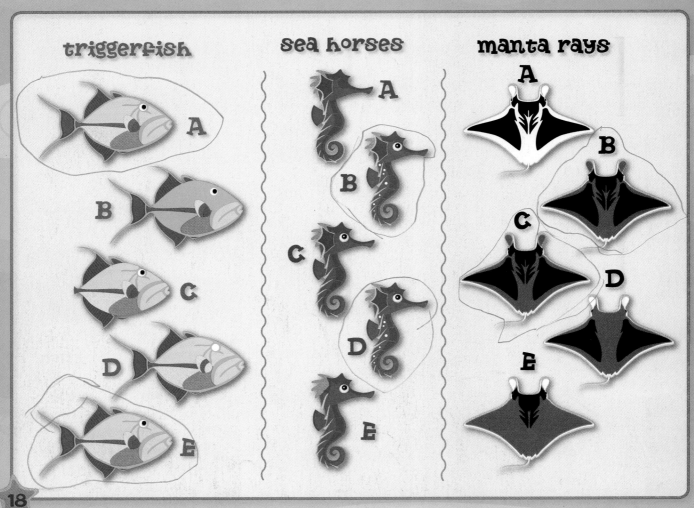

triggerfish

A

B

C

D

E

sea horses

A

B

C

D

E

manta rays

A

B

C

D

E

Chapter 4: Shape Up!

Most fish in the ocean have a pointy head and tail. This **body shape** makes it easier for fish to slip through the water. Even though most fish are narrower at their ends, they differ from each other in many other ways. Did you know that the shape of a fish can tell you a lot about where it lives? Let's look at a few fish to find out more.

yellowfin tuna

This torpedo-shaped tuna is one of the fastest fish in the sea. Tuna have very strong muscles and sharp fins tucked against their bodies. They travel in schools in the open ocean and use their incredible speed to catch squid, sardines, and other food.

starry flounder

Some fish are as flat as a pancake. This starry flounder lives on the ocean floor and hides well in the sand.

This thin pipefish is the same color and shape as the grass it lives in. Predators that might want to eat the pipefish have a hard time seeing it.

pipefish

CLOWNING AROUND!

Q: What fish do you call when your piano is out of tune?

A: A *tune*-a fish!

19

collared butterfly fish

Butterfly fish are flat, too, but they're flattened side to side, sort of like thin cookies "swimming" on their edges. Their thin, flat shape allows them to easily slip into nooks and crannies in their coral reef home.

> Those butterfly fish are shaped like me! Hey...how come they're copying me?

garibaldi

Tails can also tell you a lot about a fish. A fish with a wide tail, like this garibaldi, is not very fast. The wide tail fin has to push against a lot of water, which slows the fish down. But that doesn't matter much to the garibaldi. It eats slow-moving food (or food that doesn't move at all), and it never strays too far from its seaweed home.

You've done some great swimming and learning so far! Let's keep going and meet some other groups of fish!

Chapter 5: Lots of Other Fish in the Sea

Meet the Cartilaginous Fish

You've already discovered on page 10 that most fish in the ocean, including Dory, Tad, and me, are called bony fish. Our skeletons are made of bone—just like yours! Bruce and Mr. Ray are fish, too, but not bony fish. Their skeletons are made of cartilage, so they're called *cartilaginous fish*. Cartilage is much more flexible than bone. It's bendable like your nose and ears.

Here's a close-up look at what makes cartilaginous fish different from other fish:

Instead of scales, cartilaginous fish have tough skin made of tiny tooth-like spines called denticles.

Cartilaginous fish don't have swim bladders to help them go up and down. They have to keep moving or they'll sink. Some take rests on the bottom of the ocean.

Five or six slits lead to their gills. Bony fish have a flap of skin here instead.

Their mouths are full of several rows of teeth. When they lose a tooth, another one moves forward.

That's a Mouthful, Mate!

Fish like me, Bruce, Anchor, and all of the skates, rays, and sharks in the ocean are *cartilaginous* (car-tuh-LAH-jin-uhs) *fish*. Our skeletons are made of cartilage, not bone.

Chum
mako shark

Let's meet a few other cartilaginous fish! The stingray is one of more than 500 kinds of rays. Stingrays have at least one large, poisonous spine on their tails. Rays often rest on the ocean floor.

stingray

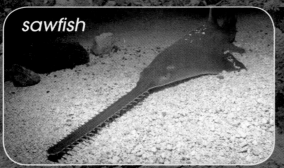

sawfish

The sawfish has a long, spiky-edged "saw" for a nose! This saw can be used to hit and injure small fish and to dig in the sand for food, such as shrimp. Their spiky nose can also be used as a weapon if they feel threatened. Watch out!

Whale sharks are the largest fish in the ocean. This shark is about as long as five cars lined up end to end. The whale shark may be huge, but it's harmless. It eats small, floating food called plankton.

whale shark

Meet the Jawless Fish

Instead of having jaws that chomp and chew (like bony and cartilaginous fish), lampreys and hagfish have round, sucking mouths with circles of tiny teeth.

lamprey

Lampreys latch onto other fish and live on their blood. They look like long snakes or giant worms. Lampreys are born in rivers, but spend most of their lives in the ocean.

Some hagfish feed mainly on sick or dying fish, while others feed on ocean worms. Hagfish ooze out slime to keep predators away.

hagfish

23

Chapter 6: A Rainbow of Fish

Purple and yellow, black and white, polka-dots and stripes...it's like a colorful costume party in the ocean! But these colors and patterns aren't just for looks—they help fish in many ways. A fish can use its colors to protect itself from predators or send messages to other fish.

Hide-and-seek

All of the crazy patterns on this triggerfish make it very hard for a predator to find it. Spots, stripes, and other patterns help it hide in its coral reef home.

clown triggerfish

pygmy sea horse in coral

There's a sea horse hiding in this coral! Can you see it? Many fish, like sea horses, hide by taking on the color, shape, or texture of their surroundings.

Is that a rock or a fish? It's a scorpion fish pretending to be a rock!

scorpion fish

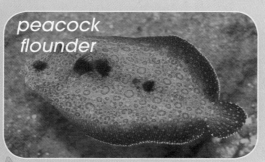
peacock flounder

Some fish can change their color to blend into their surroundings! This peacock flounder blends in well with the ocean floor.

spotfin butterfly fish

Some fish have false eyespots—shapes that look like eyes that are really near their tails. This confuses predators. They might attack the fish's tail instead of its head, giving the fish a chance to get away with a flick of its fins.

Hey, look! I have eyespots, too!

communicate in color!

When you're happy or sad, you show how you feel by smiling or frowning. Fish can't frown, but many can change the color of their skin to send messages to other fish. The color of damselfish becomes much brighter when they're looking for a mate or defending their eggs.

damselfish

That's a Mouthful, Mate!

A *parasite* (PAIR-uh-syte) is a plant or animal that lives on and harms another plant or animal.

ANCHOR
hammerhead shark

Cleaner wrasses help fish by removing *parasites* from their scales. Many fish recognize the wrasses' bright colors and swim to them for a nice, good cleaning!

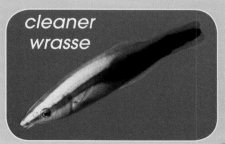

cleaner wrasse

25

Chapter 7: Keeping Fish Safe: Slime, Spines, & Stingers

clown fish

Clown fish, like my dad and I, have bright colors that shout "stay away"! The stripes warn other fish not to come near us.

We also have another special trick that keeps us safe from predators. We live in sea anemones (uh-NEH-moe-nees). Sea anemones have tentacles that can sting other fish, but not us clown fish! When we're young, the slime on our bodies mixes with the slime on the sea anemones. We get tiny little stings from the sea anemone's slime, but these little stings actually help us! As we grow up, we get used to the stings, until the stings don't harm us at all.

Not all fish sleep in a bed of stinging tentacles to stay safe! They have many other ways of defending themselves. They might...

parrot fish

...sleep in slime...

Parrot fish protect themselves at night by resting in a net of slime.

CLOWNING AROUND!

Q: How do clown fish like their eggs?

A: Funny side up!

...act like a pincushion...

Porcupine fish become a nasty—and prickly—mouthful if a predator tries to take a bite. They inflate their bodies by swallowing water. Ouch!

porcupine fish

surgeonfish

...sprout a spine or two...

Surgeonfish have two small, very sharp spines near their tails. They lash out and cut predators when threatened.

lionfish

...poke with poison...

This lionfish may be a bathing beauty, but the fringes on its fins hide poison-packed spines.

...wear a suit of armor...

Boxfish have hard scales that are joined together to make a strong box-like shell.

I'm covered in hard scales, too!

boxfish

...or swim with their friends!

Staying in school is smart for kids *and* fish! For fish, there's safety in numbers. By swimming in large groups (or schools), fish have more protection from predators.

school of salmon

Chapter 8: Fish Food!

After all this swimming, I'm feeling a little hungry. It's too bad there isn't a neighborhood diner or kitchen for fish! Fish have to snatch, stab, slurp, zap, or even spit to catch their food. And some fish even use fishing rods and lures to attract their prey! Let's take a look.

frogfish

A Fish that Fishes

One of the fins of this frogfish looks like a fishing rod with bait on the end. The fish sits quietly on the ocean floor with its rod out to attract other fish. When its prey gets close enough, the frogfish lunges!

Coral Chompers

Parrot fish have powerful "beaks" made of tiny teeth that are closely packed together. They use their "beaks" to scrape seaweed off hard coral and rocks.

parrot fish

triggerfish

Triggerfish have small, powerful jaws and sharp, cutting teeth. They use their teeth to catch and crunch up worms, snails, crabs, and coral.

super suckers

The trumpetfish uses its long snout like a straw. It hides amongst coral and then sucks up its supper—usually a smaller fish—that might happen to swim by!

trumpetfish

torpedo ray

it's shocking!

The torpedo ray is electrifying! It has special organs near its head that can create enough electricity to knock a person over. If a fish swims between the ray's "wings," it shocks and stuns the fish.

shoot with a squirt

Most of the time, archerfish feed on insects and other food in the water. But when they see food, like a spider, on a plant that's on land, they spit a stream of water! A direct hit will knock the food off the plant and into the archerfish's mouth.

Fish spend a lot of their day eating. But sometimes they have more important things to do. What could be more important than eating? Let's find out!

archerfish

Chapter 9: Fish Babies

Sometimes taking care of babies is more important than eating! Some fish are such busy parents they don't have time to eat while they guard their eggs. And fish can keep those eggs in some pretty strange places.

jawfish

Eggs-tremely careful!

Jawfish care for eggs inside their mouths! Males carry a cluster of eggs in their mouths for about two weeks until they hatch.

damselfish

Female damselfish lay their eggs in large masses in a coral reef—where they can be well hidden. Males protect their babies from danger, and even make barking sounds—like guard dogs with fins!

Male sea horses, like my dad, carry eggs in a pouch on their belly!

That's right, son!

Egg-stra Facts

Most fish hatch from an egg. Inside the egg, a tiny baby, or embryo, grows. It gets its nutrition from the egg's yolk, which is just like the yolk in a chicken's egg. Eggs can take from a few days to a few weeks to hatch.

Fish for the Future

Many fish release thousands or even millions of eggs into the water, and then just swim away. They don't provide any type of care. Other fish lay fewer eggs but care for them longer. And some fish even give birth to live babies.

A female rockfish lets her tiny eggs develop and grow inside her body. Then she gives birth to thousands of tiny, see-through, baby fish.

rockfish

egg case

Many types of sharks and rays lay large egg cases. The fish babies are protected by the tough cases. Some people who find these empty egg cases on the beach call them "mermaids' purses."

Birds aren't the only type of animal that make nests. A female salmon makes a nest at the bottom of a stream by flapping her tail to clear away a spot in the gravel. Then, she lays hundreds of red eggs, each about the size of a pea, in the nest.

salmon eggs

Siamese fighting fish

Do you like to blow bubbles? So do these freshwater Siamese fighting fish. The males blow a nest of bubbles and the females lay their eggs in the floating nest.

Chapter 10: Freaky Fish

Did you know there are fish with fangs, fish with built-in flashlights, and fish with stomachs that stretch like a balloon? The ocean is home to some pretty weird fish.

It Came From the Deep

The bottom of the ocean is cold and dark. There also isn't a lot of food down there. So fish that live in the deep sea have some tricky ways of finding their dinner. The viperfish uses a lighted lure on its fin to attract prey. When a fish swims close, the viperfish throws back its head and opens its jaw. Its long, fang-like teeth form a nasty trap. *Chomp!*

viperfish

anglerfish

Anglerfish use a built-in fishing pole that comes out of their forehead to attract fish. Fish think that the growth on the end of the pole is food. But instead of getting food for themselves, they become dinner for the anglerfish!

Dory and my dad had a scary run-in with an anglerfish! Yikes!

gulper eel

The slow-moving gulper eel has a gigantic mouth and a long, skinny body. It can make its mouth even bigger by unhinging its jaw. And it can stretch its stomach to make room for larger meals!

At night, the snake-like black sea dragon swims to the sea's surface to feed on small fish and shrimp. During the day, it stays in the deep dark. The whiskers on its chin light up to attract prey. It also flashes lights on its body to send messages to other black dragons.

black sea dragon

hatchetfish

The tiny hatchetfish is only about as long as your little finger. Its large eyes and mouth point upward. The hatchetfish scans the water above for food. Then, with its large mouth, it grabs its prey—a tasty shrimp—and gobbles it up with its sharp teeth.

Light Up My Life

Many deep-sea fish can create their own light using chemicals inside their bodies. Some of the fish you've just met use that light to attract prey. Others use it to send signals to other fish. The hatchetfish uses a row of lights on its belly to hide. When a predator looks at a hatchetfish from below, its belly will blend into a moonlit (or sunlit) sky.

Have you ever wondered why my dad and I are called clown fish? Maybe it's because people think our bright colors look like the crazy clothes a clown might wear.

Or maybe it's because we're so funny!

Let's swim to the next page to find out about some fishy names!

33

Who's Who in the Fish Zoo?

Some fish are named after other animals. Do you think a ratfish looks like a rat? Does a frogfish look like a frog? Take a look for yourself and find out!

The teeth of a ratfish look something like the teeth of a rat. But that's where the resemblance ends. Ratfish live on the ocean bottom and crush clams with their strong teeth.

ratfish

frogfish

This warty frogfish is a type of anglerfish. A better name for the frogfish would be toad fish—since it has bumps on its skin like a toad. (Frogs have smooth, slick skin.)

The cowfish is a type of boxfish. Remember the boxfish you met on page 27? Just like a cow, this fish has two horns on its head.

cowfish

elephant fish

The elephant fish uses its long snout for digging around in the mud of rivers or lakes for food. Unlike elephants, the elephant fish has tiny jaws at the end of its "nose."

Are you ready to put some of your fishy knowledge to the test? Let's take a break and play a game!

FISHY FUN: Home Sweet Fishy Home

Uh-oh! These fishies have strayed from home. Can you help them get back? Match the fish on the left (A to E) with the correct undersea home and description on the right (1 to 5). Their body shape should help you figure out where they live and hide. *(When you're done, turn to page 38 to check your answers.)*

A. sea dragon

1. sea urchin

This tiny, skinny, and pointy fish can easily hide in the spines of a sea urchin.

B. angelfish

2. rock crevices

This long, snake-like fish can lurk in caves and crevices in rocks.

C. shrimpfish

3. open ocean

These fish are fast swimmers. They live in the open ocean and are usually found in schools.

D. moray eel

4. seaweed

With its leafy fins, this fish easily blends into seaweed.

E. yellowtail kingfish

5. coral reef

Having a thin shape allows this fish to slip through a coral reef. Its bright colors also blend into a coral reef.

SHOW·AND·TELL

with Ichthyologist, Dr. Adriana Aquino

We have a new friend at Undersea School... Dr. Adriana Aquino. Dr. Aquino is an ichthyologist, which means she studies fish of all shapes and sizes. She especially likes to study catfish. Let's learn some new fishy facts from Dr. Aquino and find out about her underwater adventures!

What does an ichthyologist do?

DR. AQUINO: An ichthyologist studies the behavior of fish, what they eat, and how many fish there are in the ocean. My job is to discover and describe all the kinds of fish that live on Earth and find out what their place is in the family tree of fish. For example, in the family tree of fish, clown fish and pink anemone fish are closely related because they both live in anemones, and have similar body shapes, colors, and teeth. So, ichthyologists place clown fish and pink anemone fish in one group.

Can you tell us some interesting things about catfish?

DR. AQUINO: Catfish are one of the largest groups of fish on Earth. Ichthyologists have already discovered more than 2,200 different kinds. Most of them live in freshwater. Catfish use their whiskers to explore the things around them, just like cats do. But catfish whiskers are sensitive to touch *and* taste. Another interesting thing about catfish is that they don't have scales. Scales protect most fish from bumps and infections. Instead of scales, most catfish have slimy mucus that covers their bodies and protects them.

catfish

Where have you studied fish?

DR. AQUINO: I have gone on field trips to Argentina, Bolivia, and Brazil. However, I've studied fish from all over the world! How is that possible? I didn't have to travel around the world to study them. I've examined fish from museum collections, which are like libraries filled with information about all kinds of fish.

Can we learn about the ocean by studying the fish that live in it?

DR. AQUINO: The fish that we know about today have lived in the ocean for millions of years. So, we can learn about the history of the ocean, and the health of the ocean by studying fish.

If you could be any fish in the ocean, which would it be?

DR. AQUINO: That's a tough question. Maybe I'd be a shark! Or on second thought, maybe I'd be a cleaner fish. Cleaner fish (or cleaner wrasses—see page 25) can go inside a shark's mouth without being eaten themselves!

What kind of things do you hope to learn about fish in the future?

DR. AQUINO: I hope to better understand the family tree of the catfish I study. I'd like to learn more about all the different kinds of fish that live on Earth, so I can share with other people how amazing they are.

School's Out!

I hope you enjoyed visiting with my fishy friends! Fish really are *fin*-tastic! We've learned a lot about fish—how they breathe, swim, eat, hide, and have babies. You've met fish with polka-dots, fish covered in spines, and fish that glow in the dark.

But you haven't seen the last of your finned friends! We'll be going on lots more field trips and adventures with fish and other ocean animals—like marine mammals, reptiles, birds, and invertebrates. Just keep swimming with me, my dad, Dory, Tad, and all of our friends for more Undersea School fun!

There's one fish we didn't meet—the fish that's missing an "eye". Do you want to know its name?

Fsh! Ha-ha!

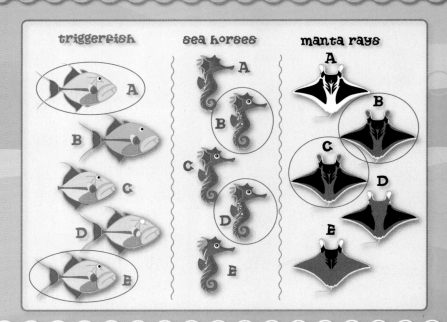

**Fishy Fun:
Fishy Look-alikes
(page 18)**

Did you find the twin fishies?

**Fishy Fun:
Home Sweet Fishy Home
(page 35)**

Did you help all the fish find their homes?

Let's see where they live...

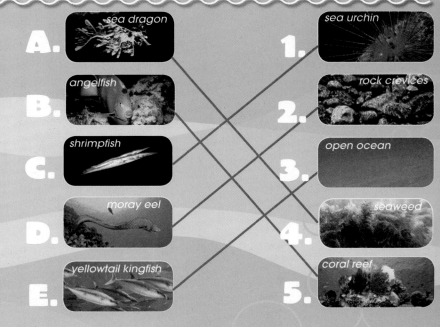

A. sea dragon
B. angelfish
C. shrimpfish
D. moray eel
E. yellowtail kingfish

1. sea urchin
2. rock crevices
3. open ocean
4. seaweed
5. coral reef